#MUMLIFE

A SNARKY ADULT COLOURING BOOK

Illustrated by Micaela

ISBN-13: 978-1533270801
ISBN-10: 1533270805

#MUMLIFE

It's 6:30 PM. By some miracle, one of your kids is asleep while the other is watching cartoons in a food coma. Quick! Here's your chance! Grab some markers, this colouring book, and run to the bathroom (don't forget the wine)! First, lock the door and enjoy the solitude of private urination. Second, gulp down that wine and enjoy the most relaxing five minutes of your day as you surrender to the quietness and creativity of colouring. Celebrate the humor and frustration that are the highs and lows of motherhood featured in the pages of this book. **#Mumlife is the best life! Happy Colouring!**

 PAPETERIEBLEU

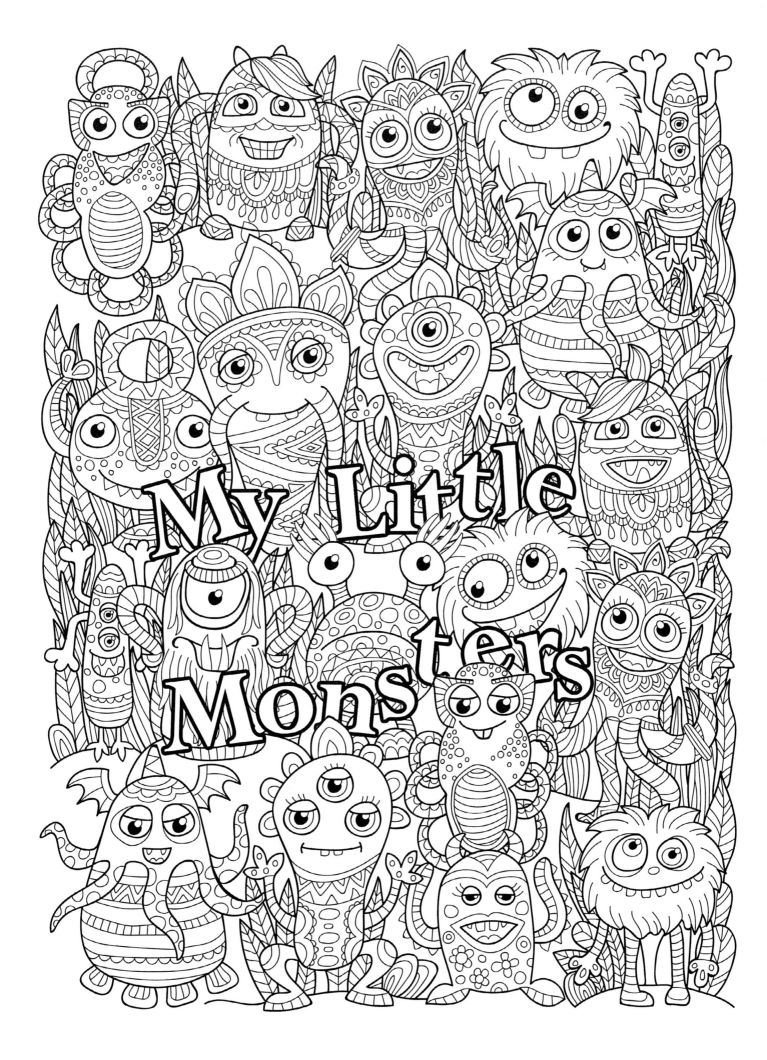

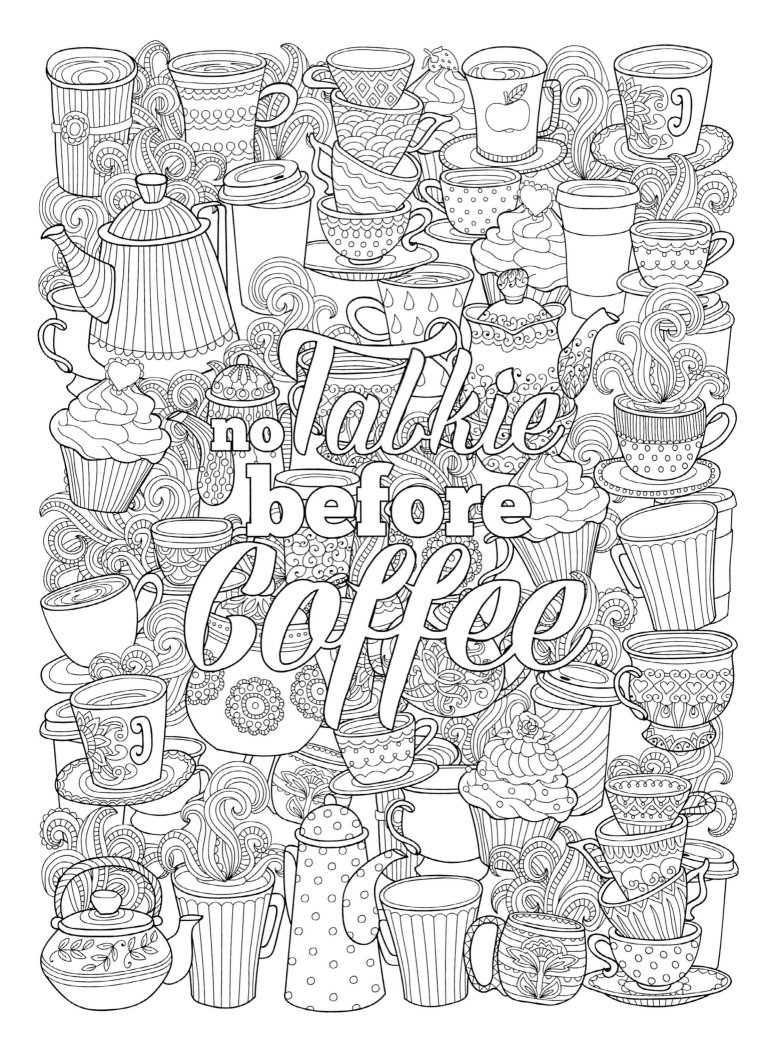

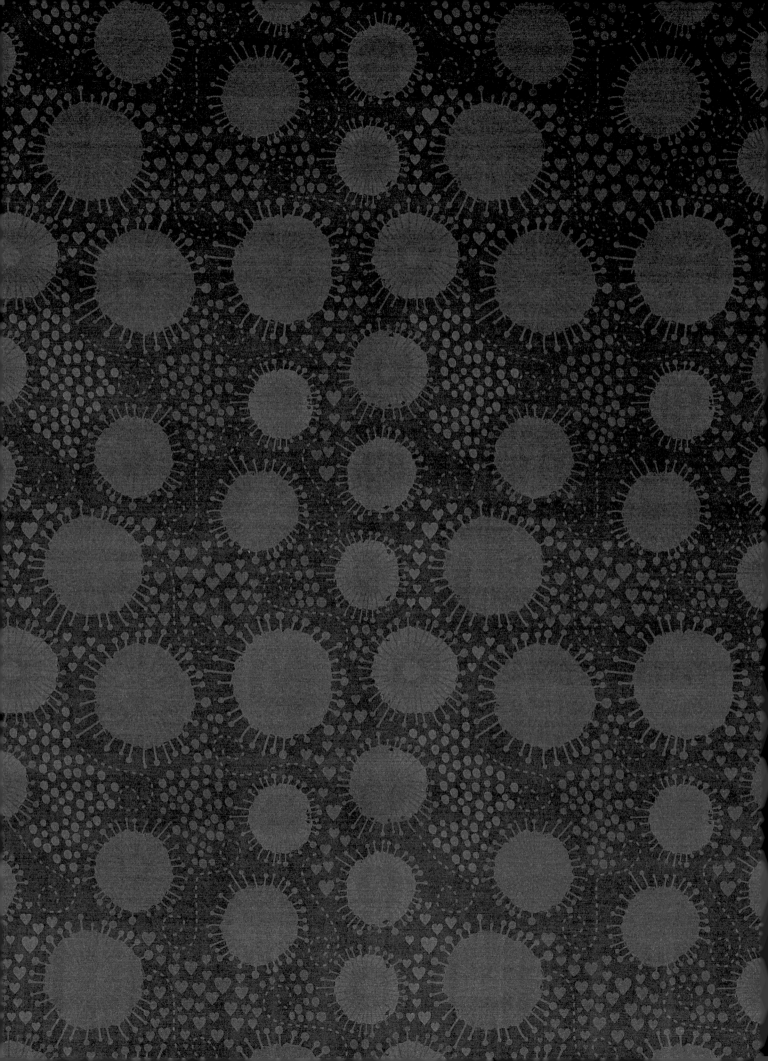

TERRIBLE TWOS

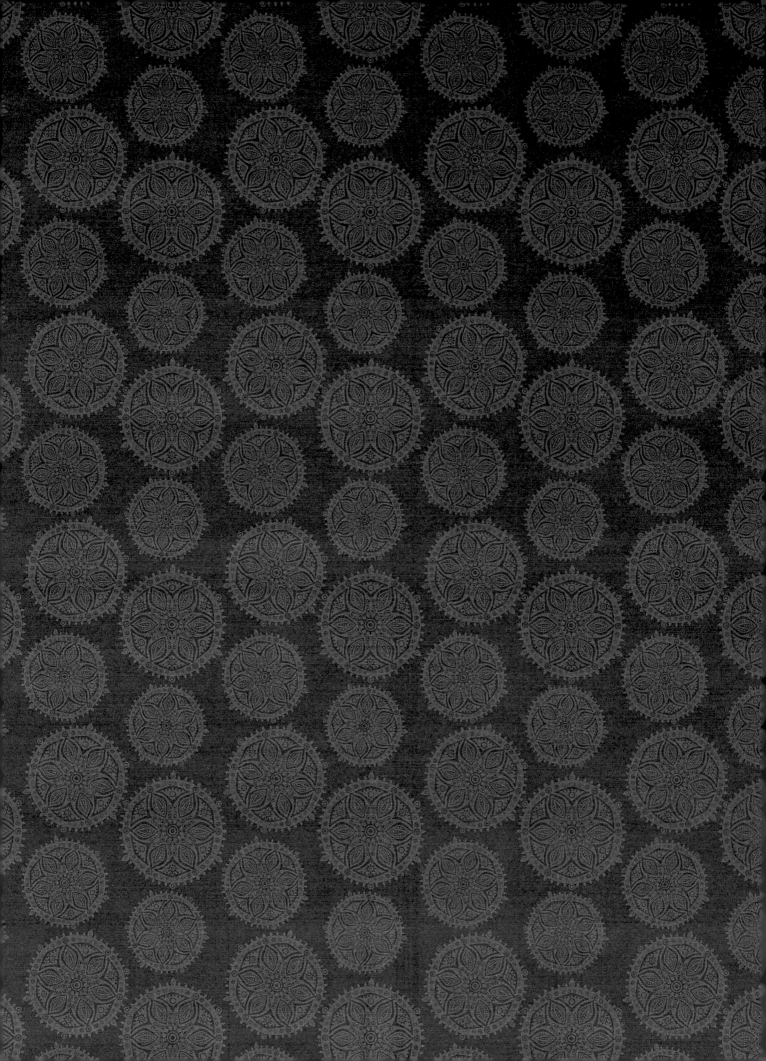

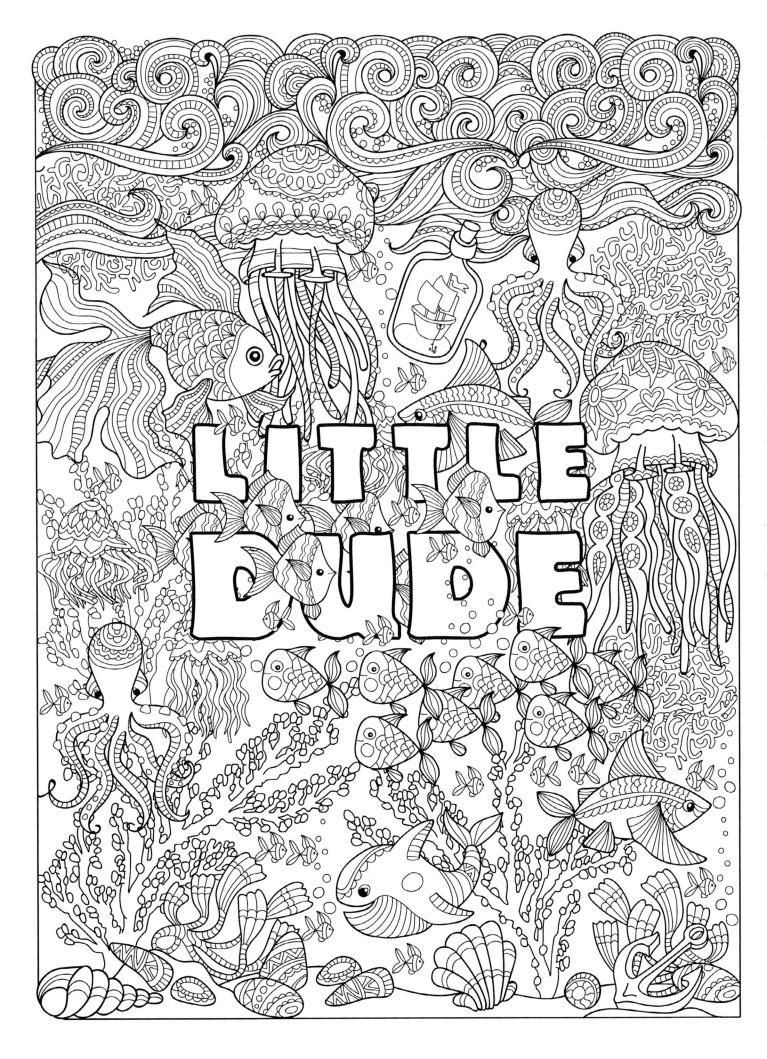

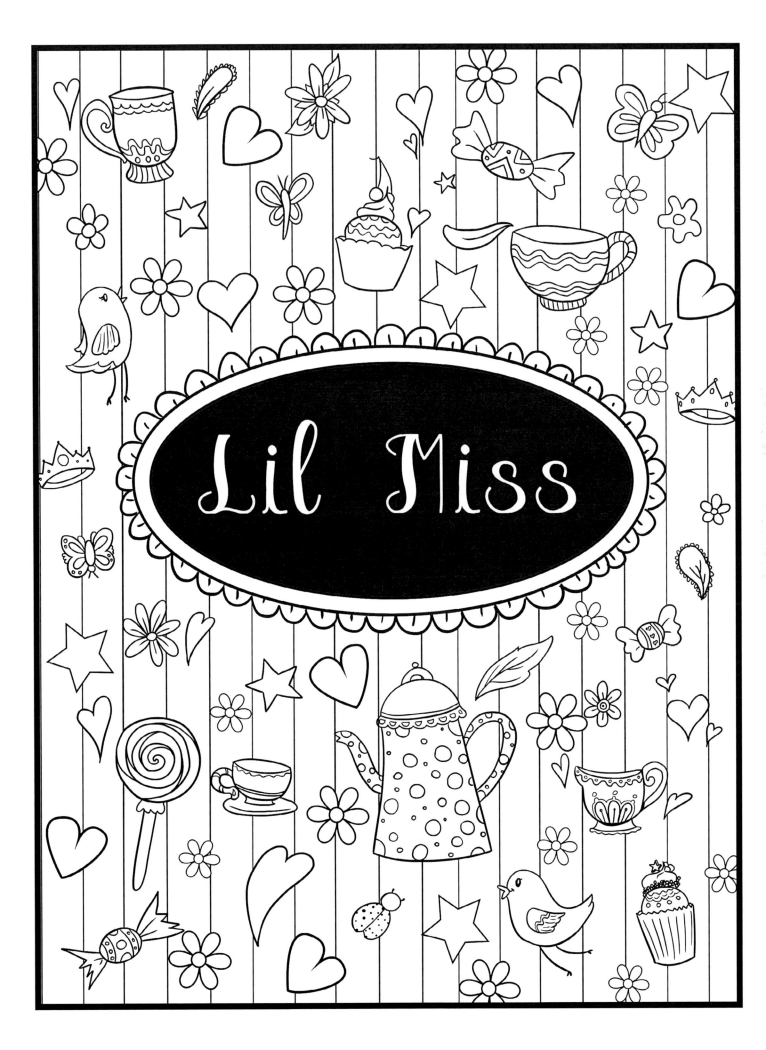

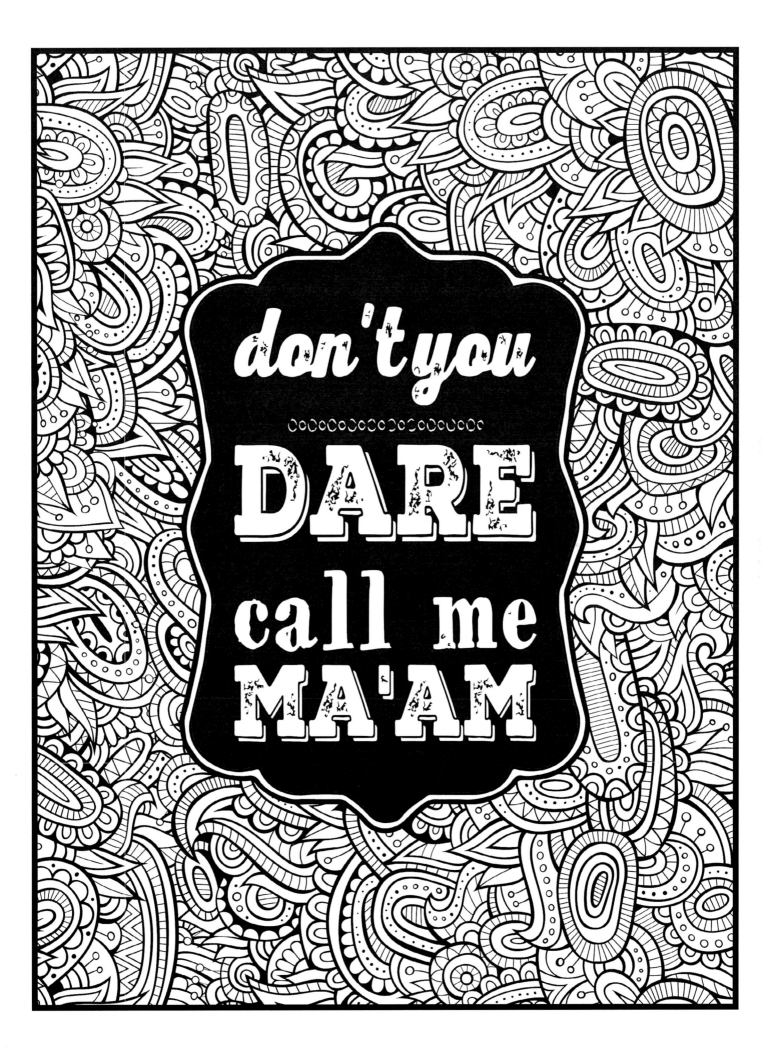

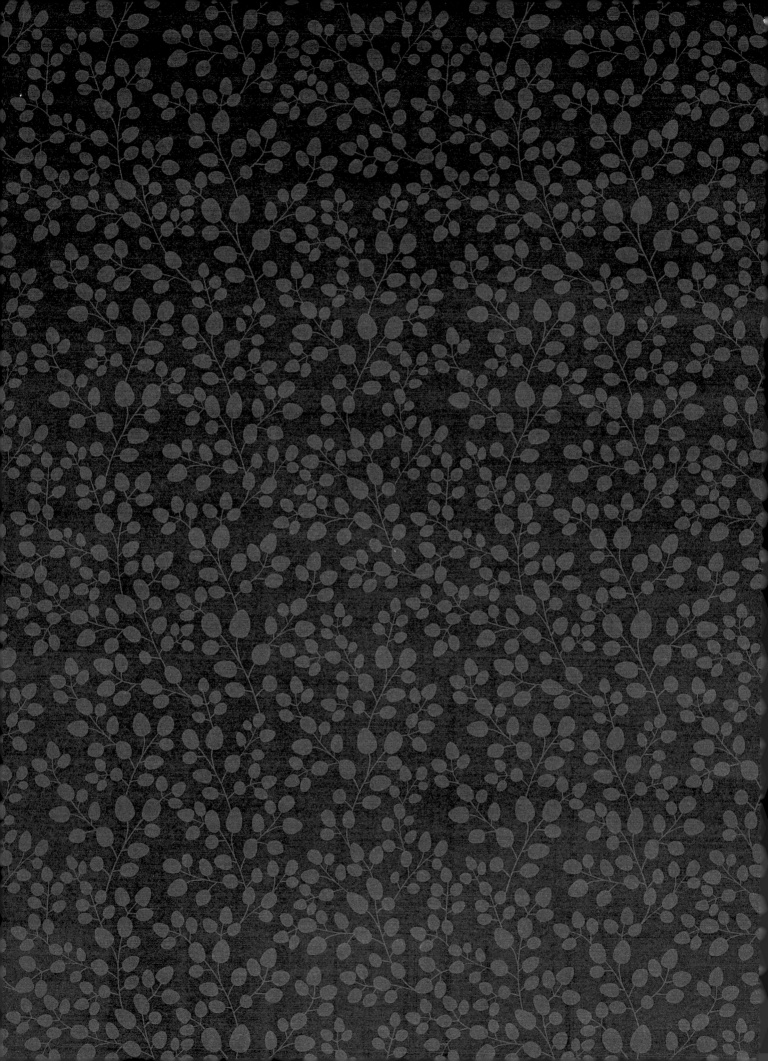

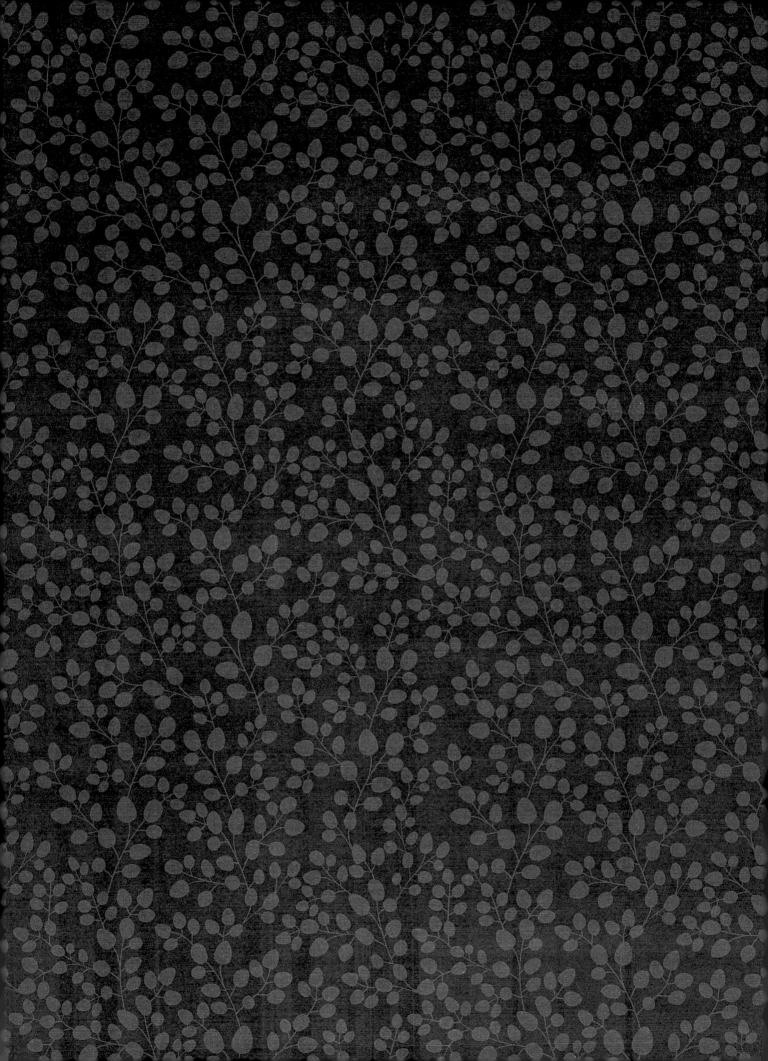

BE SURE TO FOLLOW US ON SOCIAL MEDIA FOR THE LATEST NEWS, SNEAK PEEKS, & GIVEAWAYS

@PapeterieBleu

Papeterie Bleu

@PapeterieBleu

ADD YOURSELF TO OUR MONTHLY NEWSLETTER FOR FREE DIGITAL DOWNLOADS AND DISCOUNT CODES

www.papeteriebleu.com/newsletter

CHECK OUT OUR OTHER BOOKS!

www.papeteriebleu.com

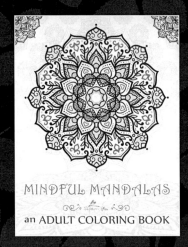

www.papeteriebleu.com

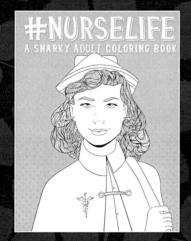

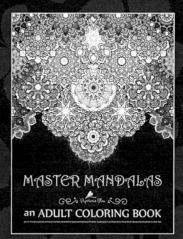

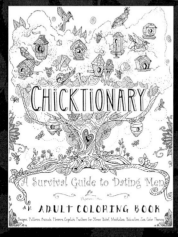